Pure

Holiness and Purity

Climbing Higher Daily Readings – Book 1

Michael Ross-Watson

DEDICATION

"This book is dedicated to my wife, Esther, to whom I have been married for 42 years. She is even easier to stay in love with than to fall in love with, and has been God's wonderful gift to me and a constant strength, encouragement and support. I owe so much to her and without her input into my life, this series of devotional books would never have been written."

Cover Photography – Used with permission
Book Layout and Preparation – KJPublishing.com

FOREWARD

Over the past few years many people have told me that I should write books. Several people have even prophesied over me about this, but somehow when I have tried to write it has been a struggle.

In mid-2014, Simon Benham, the senior pastor of Kerith Community Church where my wife and I attend asked me if I would consider writing a series of daily devotions for the church. It was like God turned a light on, and I have so enjoyed writing each day.

Each series of the daily devotions are now being put into books and will be available under a general title, "Climbing Higher."

I want to express my special thanks to Simon, who constantly encourages me. I am also grateful to Ken Jones who is helping me with the practical side of making these daily devotionals available to a wider audience.

I trust that as you read these daily words that you would hear from God and, draw nearer to Him, and be richly blessed.

Michael Ross-Watson

February 2015

CONTENTS

CALLED TO BE HOLY AS GOD IS HOLY 6

RECEIVE RIGHTEOUSNESS (HOLINESS) AS A GIFT 8

SAINTS NOT SINNERS..10

HOLINESS AND NEW BIRTH..12

THE MEANING OF NEW BIRTH 14

SANCTIFIED THROUGH AND THROUGH 16

BE WHAT GOD SAYS YOU ARE...18

CLEANSE MY HEART LORD 20

THE BEAUTY OF HOLINESS 22

GOD'S WILL IS THAT WE BECOME LIKE JESUS 24

HOLINESS AND THE HOLY SPIRIT...26

LIVING IN THE NEW WAY OF THE SPIRIT 28

HUNGRY FOR GOD..30

HOW DO I WALK IN THE SPIRIT 32

YOUR WILL NOT MY WILL 34

PERFECT LOVE..36

BE FILLED WITH THE LOVE OF GOD 38

CLEANSED BY GOD'S WORD..40

ETERNAL LIGHT..42

SHINING AS LIGHTS IN THE WORLD...44

WALK IN THE LIGHT 46

THE PURE IN HEART..48

TO THE PURE ALL THINGS ARE PURE 50

THE REFINER'S FIRE..52

THE KNIFE..54

GOD LOVES US ENOUGH TO HURT US 56

THE THREE ENEMIES OF HOLINESS 58

OVERCOMING THE WORLD...60

AN UNDIVIDED MIND 62

HOW TO DEAL WITH THE FLESH 64

SAY NO TO THE ENEMY..66

HANG IN THERE – DON'T GIVE UP 68

OUR BLESSED HOPE 70

CALLED TO BE HOLY AS GOD IS HOLY

Bible Reading: 1 Peter 1:13-25

"But just as He who called you is holy, so be holy in all you do; for it is written 'Be you holy, because I am holy'" [1 Peter 1:15-16]

We begin a series of devotionals on holiness and purity with God's command that we are to be holy, as He is holy. The best place to begin with the subject of holiness is with the Holy One – God Himself. The heavenly creatures around His throne cry "Holy, holy, holy, is the Lord of hosts. The whole earth is full of His glory" [Isaiah 6:3]. The Psalmist declares, "The Lord our God is holy!" [Psalm 99:3,6]. He is our standard and not the much lower standard of comparing ourselves with other people.

God's holiness is to be totally separated from sin. His holiness is such that He hates sin. He so hates sin that when Jesus became sin for us the Father turned His face away, and Jesus cried out from the cross, "My God, my God, why have you forsaken me" [Matthew 27:46]. The Father could not look on sin. Such is His holiness, that He demands that we too be holy, deal with sin and have that same holy hatred of sin.

Wherever God's Spirit has moved powerfully in revival, one of the first evidences of His presence is that people are convicted of sin. If we are going to be holy, then we need to have the same attitude to sin that God has. In the early church one of the key questions asked of the baptismal candidates was whether or not they had turned from sin, renounced the works of darkness and received Christ.

Questions:

We are to be holy as God is holy. What do you understand to be the meaning of God being Holy?

Would you say that in your life there is freedom from sin and a desire to constantly be pleasing to God?

RECEIVE RIGHTEOUSNESS (HOLINESS) AS A GIFT

Bible Reading: Romans 5:1-21

How is it possible that I, a sinner, could be holy as God is holy?

When Jesus died upon the cross He became sin for us. All our sins, past, present and future, were laid on Him. In taking the punishment for our sin Jesus satisfied the demand for justice of a God who is holy. The price can only be paid once. Jesus paid it all to set us free from sin.

Now when the holy God looks on us He sees us as free from sin. There is a verse of an old song that says,

> *"God sees my Saviour, and then He sees me*
>
> *In the beloved, accepted and free"*

Although we were sinners, through faith in what Jesus did on the cross we became righteous in God's sight. Righteousness is a gift to be received [Romans 5:17]

Paul says, "For He [God] made Him [Christ] who knew no sin to become sin for us, that we might become the righteousness of God in Him" [2 Corinthians 5:21]. He also writes, "You were washed, you were sanctified [set apart], you were justified in the name of the Lord Jesus Christ and by the Spirit of our God" [1 Corinthians 6:11]. This statement is in the past tense! It happened when we turned from sin to Christ.

I may not feel that I am holy, and I am certainly not perfect but I have to reckon myself righteous before God on the basis of what Jesus did on the cross. To reckon means that I count it to be true, and this requires faith.

This is so simple and yet so profound. Will you today come simply to Jesus, acknowledging that in yourself there is no righteousness, and surrender to Him, believing that as you turn in faith to Him that you become the righteousness of God in Christ – no more guilt, condemnation or fear of judgment? Free!

Questions:

1. Many people think that holiness is simply something we have to work at and do not understand that it is firstly a gift to be received. How does this thought impact you?

2. What do you think is the meaning of the phrase, "without holiness no one will see the Lord" in Hebrews 12:14?

SAINTS NOT SINNERS

Bible Reading: 2 Corinthians 5:11-21

When we turn from sin and come to Christ, we become a new creation. The Bible says that each person who has experienced this new birth is a saint. Thus Paul writes to the saints in Corinth [1 Corinthians 1:2; 2 Corinthians 1:2; Ephesus [Ephesians 1:1]; Philippi [Philippians 1:1]; and Colossae [Colossians 1:2]. The word "saints" is translated in the NIV as "holy people."

Many years ago I was preaching in a large church. During the sermon I asked the congregation to raise their hands up if they were sinners and like good sheep they all raised their hands. That was with the exception of one person, Robert, who was sitting behind me on the platform.

At the end of the meeting Robert challenged me. "Never call me a sinner again," he said. I thought that this was rather proud and retorted with a verse of Scripture – "If we say we have no sin, then we deceive ourselves and the truth is not in us" [1 John 1:8]. Robert responded by saying that he *used to be a sinner but was now a saint who sometimes sins*. I was shocked, but he explained that when he was born again God gave him a totally new nature. He was no longer a sinner but now a saint. God made him holy when he turned from sin and put his faith in Christ and was born again.

God's Word teaches us that when we are born again we receive a new nature. "Therefore, if anyone is in Christ, the new creation has come: the old has gone, the new is here" [2 Corinthians 5:17]

Questions:

1. If you have always considered that a saint is someone who is much holier than yourself, would you now begin to rethink on the basis of God's Word that says in Christ you are a saint?

2. What God says we are is an important step in becoming the person that God wants you to be. Would you thank Him today for whom He has made you to be in Christ?

HOLINESS AND NEW BIRTH

Bible Reading: 1 John 3:1-10

The first key to holiness is new birth. Holiness is not a series of negative commandments that must be obeyed but is something that happens when a person is born again. John makes it clear, "No one who is born of God will continue to sin, because God's seed remains in them; they cannot go on sinning because they have been born of God" [1 John 3:9].

It is generally understood that not to continue to sin means not to habitually and deliberately sin. It does not mean that we are sinless. If that were the case, then John would not have said to Christians in the same letter that if we do sin, then we can be forgiven and made clean [1 John 1:9] or that if we do sin Jesus stands before the Father as our advocate who pleads for us [1 John 2:1-2].

If we have been born of God then we will not habitually and deliberately choose to sin! The question then arises, what does it mean to be "born of God"?

Recently I asked a senior pastor of a large church what is the meaning of being born again. He replied that all of the person becomes new. Shocked, I asked him if the body becomes new and the answer was obviously no. Then I asked if the mind becomes new, to which he replied that it has to be renewed on a daily basis. I asked, "If the body and mind do not become new then which part of the person is born again?" He was unsure of how to answer. Many Christians seem unsure about what exactly new birth is, and yet it is a key to being holy and Jesus said that without new birth it is impossible to enter the kingdom of heaven [John 3:3,5]

Questions:

1. Tomorrow we will look more closely at the meaning of new birth. What at this moment is your understanding of new birth?

2. Why is it impossible to be holy without being born again?

THE MEANING OF NEW BIRTH

Bible Reading: John 1:10-13; John 3:1-21

Yesterday we made it clear that new birth is a key factor in Holiness, but we need to clearly define the meaning of new birth.

Nicodemus, a religious leader, came to Jesus by night. Jesus challenged him and said that unless a person is born again they can neither see nor enter the kingdom of God. Nicodemus did not understand and asked Jesus how a person could be born a second time. Jesus replied by saying that "Flesh gives birth to flesh but the Spirit gives birth to spirit" [John 3:5].

Outside of Christ the human spirit is dead towards God because of sin. The spirit is that part of man that was made to communicate with God. When we turn from sin and invite Jesus into our life, our spirit is made alive and we can communicate with God. Paul says that we become one spirit with Jesus [1 Corinthians 6:17]. The Holy Spirit makes His dwelling place in our spirit and desires that every part of our life be surrendered to Him.

We become the dwelling place of God and our body becomes a temple of the Holy Spirit. It is important that we understand that the One who has come to live inside of us through new birth is God Himself. The Holy One makes His home in our life through new birth. This is why being born again of the Holy Spirit is fundamental to holiness.

Questions:

1. New birth brings us into a relationship with God. We can then hear His voice and communicate with Him. The big question today is have you been born again?

2. Are you developing your spirit so that you can increasingly hear God's voice and enjoy His holy presence?

SANCTIFIED THROUGH AND THROUGH

Bible Reading: 1 Thessalonians 5:12-28, especially verse 23

The word translated in English as sanctified means literally 'to be set apart'. Every part of our being is to be set apart for the Lord. Our spirit, soul and body are to be kept blameless. Blameless means 'cannot be found guilty or accused'.

It is helpful to understand the difference between spirit and soul. The soul consists of the mind (intellect), will and emotions. The spirit is that part of us that was made to communicate with God and includes the conscience and intuition. Each part of our being is to be holy, set apart, and God's purpose is that we become increasingly conformed to the image of His Son, Jesus.

I have never seen such a clear difference between the spirit and the soul as I saw in a godly man in South Wales. Cyril had been a missionary in Indonesia and Thailand. He loved Jesus with all his heart, but as he grew old his body and mind began to wear out. Dementia crept in and his mind no longer functioned in the way that it had in the past. The last time we visited Cyril he barely recognized us. I suggested that we sing one of his favourite hymns, beginning with the words, "I stand amazed in the presence of Jesus the Nazarene." His mind may not have been functioning properly but as we sang Cyril sang with all his heart. Then we prayed together and Cyril prayed with such power and earnestness. His mind had gone but his spirit was so alive and bursting with love for Jesus.

Watchman Nee said that when our soul rules over our spirit, we become carnal and not spiritual, but when our spirit, made alive by the Holy Spirit rules over our soul, we become spiritual. The will of God is that each part of our being should be holy, set apart for God, spirit, soul and body.

Questions:

1. At new birth our spirit is made alive and becomes one spirit with Jesus. How can we develop our spirit man so that it becomes holy?

2. God desires that our spirit, soul (mind, will and emotions) be totally separated from sin and wholly given to Him. What does that mean to you?

BE WHAT GOD SAYS YOU ARE

Bible Reading: Ephesians 4:17-5:2

It is clear from Scripture that when a person is born again the old has gone and the new has come. Paul clearly states this in 2 Corinthians 5:17. However, for many of us there is a seeming contradiction and tension here. If we are a new creation then why do the old habits still seem to grip us and are hard to get rid of?

For many years I struggled with the concept of all things being made new, until a godly woman called me one day and asked if I had read the note in the margin of my King James version of the Bible. The verse reads, "Therefore, if any man be in Christ, *he is* a new creature; old things are passed away; behold all things are become new." My friend pointed out that in the margin the words "*he is*" in the text have the alternative rendering of "*let him be*." The meaning then is that we are a new creation but should be what we are.

Paul, writing to the Christians in Ephesus, tells them to put off the things that are wrong and displease God, and instead live a life of love as imitators of God. Writing to the Christians in Corinth, Paul speaks of the old yeast of malice and wickedness, and then says, "Get rid of the old yeast that you may be a new batch without yeast – *as you really are*" [1 Corinthians 5:6-8]. In other words, get rid of what does not honour and glorify the Lord and be what you are in Him – holy!

At conversion God declares us holy, but now there is a lifetime process of growing in holiness. Over the next few days we will look at what this growth in holy living looks like.

Questions:

1. Have you struggled with the tension of God saying you are holy but knowing that there are things in your life that are not right? How have you handled this?

2. Would you today give thanks to God for what He says you are? Now would you ask Him to help you work that out in your daily life?

CLEANSE MY HEART LORD

Bible Reading: Psalm 139:1-24

I was a young Methodist Home Missions evangelist and just twenty years old. Together with two other missioners, we went to a town in South Yorkshire for a ten-day mission. On the night that it was my turn to preach, the church was packed.

I remember that evening so well. It would be a night when my life would be deeply challenged and changed. I remember preaching on the story of the prodigal son. At the end of the message I gave an invitation for those who wanted to come to Christ. Dozens of people responded and I felt so proud that God had used me.

After the meeting I walked through the congregation, hearing some people talking and saying, "Isn't he a good preacher," and "Hasn't he got a bright future!" It was all so heady and exciting, and especially for a young man who longed to be loved, accepted and used by God.

As I shook hands with the congregation as they left that evening I was approached by Mavis. She gripped my hand tightly and looked straight into my eyes. For a moment I felt apprehension and then shock as she said, "You didn't glorify God tonight, did you? Good night!"

My pride was punctured as I went back to my lodgings that night. It was almost dawn as I crawled into bed. In His presence that night God showed me several things that were wrong in my life. There was a wrong relationship that had to be dealt with, money paid back to its rightful owner and other deep unresolved issues in my heart that had to be brought to the cross.

That was the beginning of a journey that included many such encounters, perhaps not as dramatic as that night in Yorkshire, but nevertheless God dealing with issues in my heart.

He declares us holy in Jesus but now we are on a journey of holiness, where God is changing us so that we become more and more like His son, Jesus.

Something to do:

Would you sincerely pray the prayer that David prayed, "Search me O God, and know my heart; test me and know my anxious thoughts. See if there is any offensive way in me, and lead me in the way everlasting"

[Psalm 139:23-24]? As you pray this prayer and wait quietly in God's presence let Him to show you anything that displeases Him and then seek His forgiveness.

THE BEAUTY OF HOLINESS

Bible Reading: Psalm 96:1-13

In the midst of this beautiful Psalm, extolling the greatness and righteousness of God our King we find a lovely phrase, "O worship the Lord in the beauty of holiness" [verse 9 NKJV]. The same phrase is found in Psalm 29:2 and in 2 Chronicles 20:21.

In one sense these verses point particularly to the beauty of God's holiness, but also indicate the character of holiness in general. Holiness is beautiful.

Tragically, holiness has been painted by some people as a set of negative commands to obey or a life that is devoid of fun.

Holiness is neither ugly, boring nor negative. Jesus Christ was one of the most exciting people to be with.

Many years ago I used to ride a small 75cc motorbike and used it to travel all over the country. One day everything changed – I passed my driving test and bought a car. From that day the motorbike did not come out of the shed where it was kept it until the day I sold it. Something better had come! That is how it is with holiness. We now no longer try to obey the law to make us holy because something better has come – the Holy Spirit, who lives within God's children.

A little chorus sums up the beauty of holiness:

"Let the beauty of Jesus be seen in me,

All His wonderful passion and purity;

Oh, Thou Spirit divine, all my nature refine,

Until the beauty of Jesus be seen in me."

That is holiness – the Holy Spirit working in our hearts to make us more like Jesus!

Question:

Have you been wounded by people who have spoken about holiness as only a negative set of rules to keep. Perhaps their lives did not match their words and you were put off from being the person God created you to be. Will you forgive those people and ask God to make you into the beautiful, holy person that God created you to be?

GOD'S WILL IS THAT WE BECOME LIKE JESUS

Bible Reading: Philippians 2:1-18

God's word clearly tells us that it is His will that we be conformed to the image of His Son, Jesus [see Romans 8:29]. God declares us to be holy but He is in the process of changing and refining us so that we become like Jesus [see 2 Corinthians 3:18]. The Apostle John says that when Jesus appears we shall be like Him [1 John 3:2].

There is a danger of placing the emphasis in being like Jesus in terms of the things He did and not in terms of His character. One of the pictures of the Holy Spirit is the dove. When Jesus was baptized the Holy Spirit came upon Him in the form of a dove. The wings of the dove are necessary to fly in a straight line and are perfectly symmetrical. One wing of the dove might be considered to represent the gifts of the Holy Spirit and the other to represent the fruit of the Holy Spirit. Both are necessary to live right and move forward in the Christian life. Not only does the Holy Spirit want to empower us to do the works of Jesus but also to form in us the character of Jesus.

A young boy was selling oranges from his barrow on the concourse of Grand Central Station in New York when the crowds of commuters getting off the trains knocked his barrow over. The oranges were rolling everywhere and no one seemed to care except for one kind man who stopped and began to pick up the oranges and place them back in the barrow. Through his tears the young boy asked, "Hey Mister, are you Jesus?"

Over the next few days we will take a look at how this transformation into the image and beauty of Jesus takes place in the life of a Christian.

A Question:

Holiness is becoming more and more like Jesus. Ask yourself the question, "When people meet with me do they meet with someone who is increasingly like Jesus?"

Something to Pray:

Jim Elliott, the missionary martyr to Ecuador wrote in his journal, "I want to be like a signpost at a crossroads. When people meet with me they have to make a decision." Pray that when people who are at the crossroads of life meet you, that your own life would point them in the right direction.

HOLINESS AND THE HOLY SPIRIT

Bible Reading: Joshua 5:13-15; John 14:15-27

In the Book of Joshua we read that the Lord told Joshua to take off his sandals because the place where he was standing was holy [Joshua 5:13-15]. The ground in itself was not holy, so what was it that made it holy? It was the presence of God that made the ground holy. It is God's presence in us that makes us holy.

When Jesus went back to heaven the Holy Spirit was sent to live in us and to fill us. It is His presence that makes us holy. The Holy Spirit is a beautiful Divine Person, God Himself, and He makes His home in the person who turns from their old life and sin and invites Jesus to be their Saviour. The Holy Spirit does exactly what Jesus does. Jesus said that He would send another Helper to be with us forever [John 14:16]. The word "another" in this verse is the Greek word "allos" which means "another of the same kind." Translated literally Jesus said that He would send "one besides me, and in addition to me, but just like me" [Jack Hayford].

In his theological textbook James Boyce writes, "Since the word 'allos' occurs in this text, Jesus is saying that He will send the disciples a person just like Himself, that is, one who is fully divine. Who is the first Counselor? Jesus. He had been the disciples' strength and counsel during the years of His ministry among them. Now He is going away, and in His place He will be sending a second Counselor who is just like Him. He will be another divine person living with them and [in this case] in them"

It is the Holy Spirit who works within us to change us and make us more like Jesus. He is the one who convicts us of sin, teaches us the truth and leads us in the way righteousness. He wants to fill every part of our life and makes us like Jesus.

Questions:

1. God's presence within us makes us Holy. In what way do you experience God's presence in your life?

2. The Greek word "parakletos" in John 14:16 refers to the Holy Spirit and is variously translated as Advocate, Comforter, Counsellor and Helper. He is all these things to God's children. Will you call on Him today for whatever your need may be?

LIVING IN THE NEW WAY OF THE SPIRIT

Bible Reading: Romans 8:1-39

When a person becomes a Christian, the Holy Spirit comes and makes His home in that person. That is the beginning of an amazing journey as we allow the Holy Spirit to have the control of our lives.

One of the most remarkable pictures in Scripture, is Paul's struggle with sin and trying to be holy as recorded in Romans chapter seven. In the following chapter we discover how he experienced victory over sin. What has made the difference between these two chapters? It is the Holy Spirit. Paul only mentioned the Holy Spirit once in chapter seven but in chapter eight the Holy Spirit is mentioned twenty-one times.

People who try to please God by obeying His law will constantly battle with sin and will fail. The one time Paul mentions the Holy Spirit in Romans chapter seven he writes, "...we have been released from the law so that we serve in the new way of the Spirit, and not in the old way of the written code." [Romans 7:6]. Here is a major key to living a holy life – to live and walk in the Spirit. Then we will be more than conquerors" [Romans 8:37].

What does it mean, "to serve in the new way of the Spirit?" It means to listen to and obey the Holy Spirit. The Holy Spirit gives us the power to obey God. Formerly we were "controlled" by our old sinful nature, but now we are to walk in the Spirit. Literally, the Holy Spirit now fills the believer with an internal desire to serve God.

God's promise is that the Christian who walks in the Spirit will not gratify the desires of the flesh [Galatians 5:16]. The power of the Holy Spirit is available today to turn our eyes away from our own performance and toward Jesus, and in so doing enable us to live victorious and holy lives.

Question:

Do you struggle with sin and have done your best to overcome it but feel that you have failed? Would you today ask the Holy Spirit to come and give you the power to live the way that Jesus has called you to live?

Something to Do:

Read Romans chapter 8 and underline or note every time the Holy Spirit is mentioned. Then write down exactly what the passage says about the Holy Spirit.

HUNGRY FOR GOD

Bible Reading: Psalm 84:1-12

Isaiah speaks of a longing for God [Isaiah 26:8-9]. The same longing was expressed by David in Psalm 84:2 when he wrote, "My soul yearns, even faints for the courts of the Lord; my heart and my flesh cry out for the living God" [see also Psalm 42:1-2 & Psalm 63:1].

Jesus spoke about this same longing when He said, "Blessed are those who hunger and thirst after righteousness, for they will be filled" [Matthew 5:6] and similarly in John 7:37 when He cried out, "Let any man who is thirsty come to me and drink." Jesus was speaking about the Holy Spirit [John 7:38-39]. The hungry soul who longs for righteousness will be filled with the Holy Spirit.

Many years ago I was desperately aware of my need for something more of God than I had experienced. I went to several places and spoke with different people about this longing, but was always disappointed. I was searching for about four years until one day I heard a simple Baptist preacher speaking about Paul's prayer for the Ephesian Church – "That you may be filled to the measure of all the fullness of God" [Ephesians 3:19]. I shared with this man my longing and he agreed to meet me later that evening. When we met he gave me a word of prophecy and then told me to stay where I was until the Holy Spirit filled me. Hours went by. I stood up, knelt down, and lay down repeatedly, just waiting. Then God came. He came as a bright light and overwhelmed me with His presence. I was prostrate before Him and experienced something like liquid love just filling me in wave after wave. Later that day I heard the Holy Spirit say, "That was the easy part but now walk in the Spirit!" My life has never been the same since.

Questions:

1. Charles Spurgeon, one of the greatest of preachers, said that the prayer that was most often on his lips was, "Create within me Lord a soul thirst for you." Would you today ask God to give you a hunger and thirst for Him?

2. God has made it clear that we should seek Him but sometimes it is a real battle. What are some of the things that hinder you from seeking God?

HOW DO I WALK IN THE SPIRIT

Bible Reading: Galatians 5:13-26

Living this life of holiness requires that we walk in the Spirit. "So I say, walk by the Spirit and you will not gratify the desires of the flesh" [Galatians 5:16].

To walk in the Spirit we must firstly, *live in right relationships with others*. Paul says that we are to serve one another humbly in love [Galatians 5:13]. Just as God Himself reaches out to us in love, so we are called to reach out to others. It is far easier to hear the voice of the Holy Spirit when we are reaching out to bless others.

Secondly, *deal with issues of sin in our lives*. The fruit of the Spirit is stated in Galatians 5:22-23 but interestingly in the same chapter is a list of the sins of the flesh in Galatians 5:19-21. We are to live crucified with Christ. It is good to be sensitive to the Holy Spirit and deal with any area of sin in our lives. In the words of James Hudson Taylor, we must keep short accounts with God.

Thirdly, *spend time quietly in God's presence* listening for His voice. Dare I suggest that busyness may be one of the greatest hindrances to hearing God's voice? It is the birthright of the Christian to hear God's voice [see John 10:4 and Romans 8:12]. A speaker at the Keswick Convention once gave this piece of advice – "The very next thing that God tells you to do, do it and keep on obeying Him until you meet Him face to face."

Fourthly, *spend time reading God's word*. Jesus said that we are sanctified by the truth and that His word is truth [John 17:17]. God's words are spirit and will strengthen our spirit. The Psalmist said, "I have hidden your word in my heart that I might not sin against you" [Psalm 119:11]. God will never tell us do something that is opposed to what He has said in His word.

Finally, *spend time in worship and praise*. Worship is for our benefit because it brings God's presence. God inhabits the praises of His people [Psalm 22:3]. It is far easier to hear God's voice and be led by the Holy Spirit when we spend prime time worshipping Him.

Question:

As you have read today's devotional word, what has God been saying to you? Is there some action you need to take?

A Prayer:

Lord, as I took short, faltering steps and often fell when I learned to walk physically, so help me to walk in the Spirit and to become stronger as I learn to trust You more and more. In Jesus Name, Amen.

YOUR WILL NOT MY WILL

Bible Reading: Matthew 26:36-46; Romans 12:1-2

Surrendering your will to God and dying to your own will and desire is one of the greatest struggles that we face. It is easy to sing, "I want God's way to be my way" but living it out is another matter. As a man, it was a struggle even for Jesus, as in the Garden of Gethsemane he sweat drops of blood and asked the Father to take the cup of suffering from Him. Nevertheless, He prayed, "Not my will but yours be done."

When speaking about dying to our own will, we are speaking about every part of our life. This is an issue of holiness. How much is Jesus Lord of my life? Is He Lord of my decision about where I live? Who I marry? Where and how I serve? How I use my money? He is Lord of every part of my life? Hudson Taylor of China wrote, "If Jesus is not Lord of all, then He is not Lord at all."

I first heard about Noby Jo from Selwyn Hughes, although her testimony is well known and documented. Noby Jo went into the hills in China to pray and as she did so the Lord showed her a different direction for her life than what she would have chosen. Annoyed, she complained to the Lord, "Why do you always have your way; what about my way for a change?" The Lord replied, "It is not that your way is wrong; it is rather that My way is best." As she surrendered her will to Him, she clearly heard the Lord say to her, "You belong to the discouraged and broken people who commit suicide at the bend of the railway track."

Noby Jo was confused by this message, but made some enquiries and discovered that outside the town where she lived was a notorious spot at the bend of the railway track where people intent on committing suicide would throw themselves over a cliff into a deep ravine. She put up a sign near the spot with these words, "**DON'T: SEE MRS NOBY JO FIRST. GOD LOVES YOU.**" She added her address and on the very first day that the sign was put up, several people knocked on her door in response to the message. Noby Jo died at the age of 92, having saved 5,000 people from suicide.

So many people were blessed because someone had died to her own desire and surrendered her will to the Lord. His way is best!

Two Things to Do:

Describe in your own words what, "Not my will but your will" means.

Ask the Lord to show you where you have not surrendered your will to Him, and then ask for His forgiveness and begin to do what He tells you.

PERFECT LOVE

Bible Reading: 1 John 4:7-21; 1 Corinthians 13:1-13

"*Love has been perfected* among us in this: that we may have boldness in the day of judgment: because as He is, so are we in the world. There is no fear in love; but *perfect love* casts out fear, because fear involves torment. But he who fears has not been made *perfect in love*" [1 John 4:17-18 NKJV]

On one occasion, when asked the meaning of holiness, John Wesley replied, "It is perfect love."

The devil has done everything he can to confuse people as to the meaning of love. The media and Hollywood have confused and misled many people by giving a wrong conception of love. Writing to the Corinthians, Paul explains what love is.

Love is **Essential** [1 Corinthians 13:1-3]. The gifts of the Holy Spirit are wonderful blessings to serve God more effectively, but without love they are merely empty sounds and without value. Even sacrifice or martyrdom gains a person nothing if love is not the motive.

Love is **Expressive** [1 Corinthians 13:4-7]. The list of the characteristics of love is remarkable.

Love is **Eternal** [1 Corinthians 13:8-13]. Love is greater than faith and hope. God is the God who gives faith and hope, but He is love [1 John 4:8,16]. One day we will not need faith or hope. We will have received what we believed for and hoped for, but love will still be there because God is love and love never fails. To be filled with love is to be filled with God!

Holiness is being filled with love and love is God!

Question:

How would you explain what love is to someone who has been confused by the way the media or Hollywood have defined love?

Something to Do:

Read 1 Corinthians 13:4-7 and note or underline the characteristics of love as defined by Paul. When you have done, this pray about how each of those characteristics might be developed in your own life.

BE FILLED WITH THE LOVE OF GOD

Bible Reading: Romans 5:1-11; Matthew 22:34-40

Jesus said that the greatest of all the commandments is to love God and to love your neighbour.

Love is the fruit of the Spirit [Galatians 5:22-23]. One commentator says that love is the sum total of all the other aspects of the fruit of the Spirit.

Jesus commanded us to love! The response to a commandment is not an emotion but a decision of the will. Have you noticed how difficult it is to love some people and especially those who have hurt us or rub us up the wrong way? Love is first of all a choice.

Esther and I gave our lives to serve Jesus. We lived on a fanatical Muslim island where there were very few Christians. One day, cycling to a village about five miles from where we lived, I challenged Esther to a race, and was soon well ahead of her. I was almost out of sight when I heard her scream. Looking back I saw that several young men had pulled her off her bike and were pulling her clothes off.

I ran back towards Esther, and as they saw me the young men ran off. Esther was deeply traumatized and in the weeks that followed often had nightmares and would cry out. She was fearful and wanted to go home to her mum. She blamed all Indonesians for what had happened. Our missionary future was clearly threatened.

Some weeks later Esther prayed a desperate prayer. "Lord, I cannot love these people, but I know You do, and I want You to love them through me." Shortly after praying Esther felt as though a bucket of warm water was being poured over her, and every part of her was being washed clean. A new love came for Jesus and for the Indonesian people. A few days later we read together, ""God's love has been poured into our hearts through the Holy Spirit, who has been given to us" [Romans 5:5].

Questions:

1. Ruth Graham said, "You cannot genuinely pray for someone and have a wrong attitude towards them." Is there someone who has hurt you, who God wants you to forgive and then to love through you?

2. In Galatians 5:23, after listing the fruit of the Spirit, Paul says, "Against such things there is no law." What do you think this means?

CLEANSED BY GOD'S WORD

Bible Reading: Psalm 119:9-16 & Psalm 119:105-112

Psalm 119 is a meditation on the excellences of the Word of God. Throughout this longest of the Psalms, the Word of God is constantly referred to as His law, statutes, word, testimony, commandments, and precepts. Very early in the Psalm we read of God's Word that cleanses us [verse 9] and keeps us from sin [verse 11]. Jesus said, "You are already clean because of the word I have spoken to you" [John 15:3]. God's Word has the power to make us clean, to keep us clean and to keep us from sin.

As a young Christian I was encouraged to read God's Word every day, and I read the whole Bible several times in my early Christian life. Much of it was without real understanding, but as I read it something was happening in my heart. The word of God is like a seed sown and then watered by the Holy Spirit.

A Christian leader from Hungary shared with me a remarkable testimony of the power of God's word to bring sin to the surface in his life. One day, as he was reading in Deuteronomy, he read of a particular sexual sin, and as he read he began to think about this sin and enjoyed the thought of it. What he was dwelling on and enjoying was not good, but he recognized that God's Word had revealed within him a root of sin that he had been previously unaware of. My friend, Otto, immediately confessed that sin, the root was removed and he was set free. That is the power of God's word to bring light, and to purify us on this journey of Holiness.

Questions:

Can you remember a time in your life when God's Word has specifically brought to the surface of your life something which was unclean and of which you needed to be set free?

Something to Do:

God's Word, the Bible is very powerful. Someone has said, "God's Word will keep you from sin, or sin will keep you from God's Word." Would you make a commitment today, with God's help, to read the Bible consistently every day? There are many daily Bible reading plans and notes available. Keep a journal of what you read, and what God speaks into your heart, and see the change that will have taken place after only one year.

ETERNAL LIGHT

Bible Reading: 1 John 1:1-10; Ephesians 4:17-5:20

John, writing his first letter, makes a declaration that God is Light and in Him there is no darkness [verse 6]. Light and darkness are two opposite ends of a spectrum. Darkness describes sin, evil and the kingdom that is ruled over by Satan. Before we came to Christ and received His salvation, we were in darkness. The god of this world blinded our minds and we could not understand truth. Describing our new position in Christ as His children, the Apostle Paul says that we have been rescued from the kingdom of darkness and brought into the kingdom of the Son he loves [Colossians 1:13]. The previous verse states that we are now God's people in the kingdom of light.

Light symbolizes honesty and purity. To "walk in the light" means to leave behind the things of our former darkness. No more hidden, selfish agendas. No more hypocrisy and dishonesty. No more pretense or play-acting.

Writing to the Ephesians Paul says, "...you were once darkness, but now you are light in the Lord. Live as children of the Light" [Ephesians 5:8]. In Ephesians 4:17 through to 5:20, Paul gives instructions for Christian living and the heart of his message is living in the light. We are to expose the fruitless deeds of darkness. Among some of those fruitless deeds of darkness are lying [Ephesians 4:25]; anger [4:26]; stealing [4:28]; unwholesome talk [4:29]; bitterness and malice [4:31]; sexual immorality [5:3].

The result of allowing the "deeds of darkness" to exist in our lives is that we sleep spiritually! Let us awake and let Christ shine on us [Ephesians 5:14]. Holiness is to live in the light!

Something to do:

Write down the negative works of darkness that Paul mentions in
Ephesians 4:17-5:20. I have mentioned some of them but there a
number of others. Then write down the positive things, that Paul says
are a part of walking in the light. Finally, write down each specific
commandment that you read in this passage.

A Question:

What has the Holy Spirit revealed to you today, as you have read this
passage in Ephesians, about walking in the light? Is there anything that
you need to change in your life?

A Prayer:

Help me to put on today my new self, created to be like God in true
righteousness and holiness. Shine your light into my heart today.
Through the power of your Holy Spirit let me please You today. In Jesus
Name. Amen.

SHINING AS LIGHTS IN THE WORLD

Bible Reading: Philippians 2:12-18; Acts 9:36-41

We are called by Jesus to let our light so shine before men that they may see our good works and give glory to God. The evidence that a person is living in the light is good works. The danger is that we get the order wrong! It is not that we do good in order to shine but that the Holy Spirit within us shines out and the result is good works.

One of the most saintly people I have ever met was my mother-in-law. Gladys admitted to being lazy at school and as she grew up she was illiterate. Gladys and her husband, Sid, came to Christ in 1939. Sid never went on with the Lord, but Gladys' life was totally transformed.

Sid complained, was moody and a gambler. He would give Gladys money for housekeeping but then steal it back to fund his gambling habit. But it would be very difficult if his wife did not continue to put meals on the table. Sometimes he locked her in the house so that Gladys could not go to church, and on at least one occasion she escaped through a downstairs window. Never once did Gladys complain or fight back, and when he was 80 years old Sid finally came to the Lord.

In those difficult years Gladys would rise in the early hours to pray. On one amazing day God miraculously taught her to read and His Word became a treasure to her. One day when there was no food in the house and no money, she and her two daughters knelt down to pray. Gladys knew the consequences she faced if there was no food on the table when her husband came home. Whilst they were praying there was a knock at the door, and a member of the church stood there with a large box of groceries. "God told me early this morning to go to the shop and buy you a box of groceries," she said.

Gladys was a light that shone brightly. As a young girl my wife saw two very different examples in her parents and made a decision to follow her mother's example, and as result countless numbers of people have been blessed. My wife is the fruit of the light of Jesus shining in her mother's life.

Questions:

1. How does Jesus want the light to shine in a difficult situation that you might face today?

2. Dorcas was known for the kind things that she did for others and for helping the poor, and as a result she and many others were blessed. How is God asking you to be kind and help the poor and thus to shine for Him?

WALK IN THE LIGHT

Bible Reading: Romans 13:1-14; 1 John 1:7

God is light and walking in the light is an important aspect of purity and holy Christian living. As we saw yesterday light is a symbol of honesty and purity. The darkness hates the light. To walk in the light is to walk right! Honesty makes us vulnerable but it is powerful. No cover up, no pretense, no trying to be something that we are not, and no hidden agendas. When Jesus met Nathaniel [John 1:47] He said, "Behold an Israelite in whom there is no guile." The words "no guile" literally mean pure and free from deceit.

To walk in the light is the basis of Christian fellowship. The apostle John says, "If we walk in the light we have fellowship one with another" [1 John 1:7]

If we are not honest then we cannot be trusted and trust is a fundamental component of any relationship. Any good relationship requires four basic elements to grow. These are love, trust, respect and understanding. Trust is the part of a relationship most difficult to be restored if it has been broken.

To walk in the light is the key to progressive cleansing from sin. John continues, "...and the blood of Jesus Christ cleanses us from all sin" [1 John 1:7]. The life of fellowship is a life that is continually cleansed from sin by the blood of Jesus. When a Christian walks in the light their lives will be known, and will not contain hidden sins, falsehoods or deception. In that openness they will experience progressive cleansing from all sin.

To walk in the light provides protective armour in spiritual battle. Light is a weapon. Where light shines it exposes the enemy and evil. Writing to the Roman Christians, Paul says that we are to put on the armour of light [Romans 13:12]. Holy and right living protects us from many dangers.

Questions:

1. Have you ever tried to have fellowship with someone you find it hard to trust? What exactly was it that made fellowship so difficult with that person?

2. In what way do you think that walking in the light is protective weapon for the Christian? Can this principle also be true for the person who is not a Christian?

THE PURE IN HEART

Bible Reading: Matthew 5:1-12; Psalm 24:1-10

Jesus said that the pure in heart are blessed [Matthew 5:8]. The word blessed used by Jesus in the beatitudes of Matthew 5:3-10 means happiness of the highest kind, and even more that, of God's special favour towards His people. The happiest people on earth are those whose hearts are pure. Sin makes a person miserable but purity of heart and the beauty of holiness make a person happy.

The Bible says that God is good to those whose hearts are pure [Psalm 73:1]. Paul, writing to Timothy exhorted him to keep himself pure [1 Timothy 5:22] and to be an example of purity [1 Timothy 4:12]. One of the conditions for entering into God's presence is to have a pure heart [Psalm 24:4].

The Greek word translated as pure in Matthew 5:8 is a word like that used for clear water, metals without alloy and of grain that has not been winnowed [that is freed from mixture of other particles].

To have a pure heart does not mean it is without sin, but it is consciously free from known sin. One day a little girl was upset when her mother came home soaked to the skin by heavy rain. The mother went upstairs to get a hot bath, and the little girl really wanted to help her mother. Suddenly she had an idea – she would dry mother's shoes in the oven. Mother, in the bath suddenly could smell burning leather and quickly came to the kitchen. As she opened the oven thick smoke began to pour out and there were her shoes, a burnt offering! Just as mother was about the explode the little girl said, "Mummy, I dried your shoes for you!" The little girl's heart was pure but not necessarily without fault. We may not be conscious of sin, and our heart may be pure, but it does not necessarily mean that we are faultless.

An old pastor once said to me that holiness is not the inability to sin, but the glorious ability not to sin.

Questions:

1. It is critical to the Christian life how we handle those who criticize us. Have you sought to do what is right, with a pure heart, and the result has not turned out as you expected? How did you handle the criticism?

2. Jesus says that purity is one of the keys to the highest form of happiness. "Self-gratification never brings satisfaction." Putting these two statements together what do they say to you?

TO THE PURE ALL THINGS ARE PURE

Bible Reading: Titus 1:10-16; Philippians 4:8

One of the evidences of purity of heart is the way that we look at things and perceive them. Writing to Titus, Paul said, "Everything is pure to those whose hearts are pure." He is writing this after making one of the most remarkable statements in God's Word. Paul has just commanded Titus to sternly rebuke the Cretan believers who often tell lies, and have a tendency to be cruel and lazy.

Even more than this there are people who rebel against the truth and with useless talk deceive others. People have been turned away from the gospel by their false teaching, and as is so often the case, the desire for money is at the root of much of this evil. Paul is emphasizing that to people who are corrupt and unbelieving nothing is pure! They have even lost the ability to discern what is pure. Their conscience has been defiled.

Paul is saying that some people see good all around them, while others see nothing but evil. Our souls become filters through which we see good and evil. People whose hearts are pure, because Jesus controls their lives, learn to see goodness and purity even in this evil world. To these people God gives the ability to discern what is right and wrong

Whatever you choose to fill your mind with will affect the way you think and act. As we meditate upon God and His Word, we will discover more and more goodness, even in this world that is so filled with violence and sin. Someone has said, "A mind filled with good has little room for what is evil."

Writing to the Philippians, Paul says that they should focus their minds on things that are pure. We are to literally fill our minds with things that are lovely, pure, praiseworthy, true, admirable and honourable.

A Question:

In this media age there is much that can become the wrong focus for our minds and our eyes. Is there an area of your mind that needs to set free from impurity? If this is the case, bring this issue to the Lord for cleansing. If it is something that is hard to break free from, then seek a Christian you trust and share your struggle with them so that you can pray together.

A Prayer:

Lord, renew my mind so that I focus on things that are pure and pleasing to You and so that I will know what You want and find how pleasing and perfect Your will really is. In Jesus Name. Amen.

THE REFINER'S FIRE

Bible Reading: Malachi 3:2-3

God sees us as already holy and fully accepted in Jesus, but desires to make our lives increasingly like His Son Jesus. To be holy is obviously more than God declaring us holy. It is a journey. If we were already perfect we would not need to put off what is the old nature and continually put on the new nature [see Ephesians 4:22-24]. There would be no need to grow in grace [2 Peter 3:16] and John would not have to write, "if any man sin" [1 John 2:1].

In order to purify us God allows us to go through trials that refine us. In Malachi we see a picture of the Lord as a refiner. The refiner heats the fire until the dross in the precious metal rises to the surface and then he scoops off that dross and impurity from the metal. It is said that he does this until the precious metal is so pure that he can see his face perfectly reflected in the metal.

Christ comes as the purifier and refiner of His people. His goal is that we should be increasingly pure until one day we are totally conformed to the image of Jesus. Whilst going through this earthly journey this is an on-going process, but one day we shall be like Him [see 1 John 3:3].

The trials that we go through to refine us are not easy and it almost seems as though they get tougher the longer we walk with the Lord. Remember that the ultimate test for Abraham was the call to give his own son as an offering to the Lord. He was one hundred and twenty years old when that test came!!

Questions:

1. God's Word says that trials are important because our character is changed for the better when we go through trials [see Romans 5:3-5]. What particular trial have you been going through recently and what has God been teaching you in the trial?

2. The testing of our faith produces patience and leads us to spiritual maturity [James 1:2-4]. Our attitude to this testing should be joy because of what it produces in us. Will you now begin to be joyful and thank God for the refining that He is taking you through?

THE KNIFE

Bible Reading: John 15:1-8

Christ is the refiner who is purifying His children. Another picture of His work of making us holy is Christ's pruning of the branches of a tree, so that the tree produces more fruit. Each of God's children is a branch that has been engrafted into Jesus who is the vine and His desire for us is that we bear much spiritual fruit.

There are areas in all our lives where we are not bearing the beautiful fruit of the Spirit in the way that God intends. These areas are not necessarily bad things that we do but are a hindrance to fruit bearing. Sometimes the good is the enemy of the best! Notice in the passage for today that there is fruit [v2], more fruit [v2] and much fruit [v8].

Jesus is the one who prunes but we allow Him the right to do so by yielding to His pruning knife. He wants to cut away from our lives anything that does not glorify Him.

This pruning process is evident in nature. I saw a gardener pruning a rose bush so harshly that I questioned whether it was the right thing to do. He cut the bush right down to almost ground level. All the greenery was gone and only a stem protruded above the ground. He told me that in order for this rose bush to have the most beautiful and abundant flowers it needed to be pruned, and the following year there were so many beautiful flowers.

We are already clean through God's Word [v3]. Righteousness is ours, but the knife is still necessary. Every part of my life must come under His scrutiny. Lord, make me willing to let go of anything that is a hindrance to the fruit You want in my life - that beautiful fruit of love, joy, peace, patience, kindness, goodness, faithfulness, gentleness and self-control.

Questions:

1. Is it your desire to bear more fruit for Jesus? If so allow Him the right to search every part of your life and take away whatever is a hindrance, however good it might be, so that you are increasingly fruitful.

2. Dr. A.W.Tozer said, "It is doubtful whether God can bless a man until He has hurt him deeply." What do you think about this statement?

GOD LOVES US ENOUGH TO HURT US

Bible Reading: Hebrews 12:3-11; Genesis 32:22-32

God as refiner purifies us and as the gardener prunes us, but there is still another picture of God who works in our lives to make us more holy. It is the picture of a father who chastens and disciplines his children.

God is a good Father. He corrects us, and sometimes has to punish us [Hebrews 12:6 NLT]. God's discipline is always right and good for us because it means that we will share in His holiness.

As a father I realize how important discipline was for my children. It was not easy because I knew it was hurting them and it was painful for me to administer discipline, but without it they would have grown up without boundaries and understanding of right and wrong. No discipline is easy — it is painful. God, as our loving Father, disciplines us so that there will be a harvest of right living for us who have been trained by Him.

Jacob had an experience of God but somehow not much had changed in his life. He was still a selfish man who deceived and cheated others. God waited for nearly twenty-five years to deal with Jacob. We read the account of God dealing with him in Genesis 32:22-32.

On the morning of that day Jacob met with angels. God was preparing him. In the afternoon he had news that his brother Esau was coming to meet him with four hundred men. Jacob was afraid because he had cheated his brother. He decided to try and protect his family and possessions by sending them over to the other side of the river.

Then God came and met Jacob. It was in a place where Jacob was alone. All the props that he had leaned were gone. It was a place of brokenness as he wrestled all night with God, and finally the Lord touched Jacob's thigh and put it out of its socket. No more running now, and weakness in place of strength! It was a place of desperation as Jacob was now clinging and crying out, "I will not let you go unless you bless me!" Finally, it was a place of honesty. "What is your name?" "Jacob," he replied. Jacob means cheat. God loved Jacob enough to hurt him and discipline, but a new Jacob had emerged. A new name – Israel! A new vision – he had seen God face to face and He could never be the same!!

Questions:

1. Some people think of God as a big softy, but He is a loving Father, who disciplines us to make us holy! How do you think God disciplines us today as His children?

2. What principles can you see in the way in which the Lord dealt with Jacob and corrected him?

THE THREE ENEMIES OF HOLINESS

Bible Reading: James 4:1-17; 1 John 2:15-17

An important key to purity and holy living is learning to say "No!" to the enemies of purity. The enemies of the Christian are not flesh and blood, but spiritual. The Bible uses three words to describe these enemies. They are the world, the flesh and the devil. All three attack in different ways and interact together.

The world is not just wrong places to go or wrong things to do – it is a spirit. It is an invisible yet surrounding atmosphere in which we live, and which erodes faith, dissipates hope and corrupts love!

The flesh is the world within us, that demands our rights, wants to rule where God should be enthroned. It is the self-life that demands gratification and says that its way, not God's way, is the best. However, as someone has declared, "Self-gratification never brings true satisfaction."

The devil is the ruler of a world system opposed to God. He was an anointed archangel in heaven but his downfall was pride – he wanted to take the place of God! He rules over his evil system through fear and control.

These three enemies are different but function together. The Bible teaches us how to handle each of them and we will look at how to handle each of these enemies over the next few days. We are to be transformed be the renewing of our mind so that we are not conformed to the world. We are to put to death, with help of the Holy Spirit, the works of the flesh, and we are to resist the devil and he will flee from us. For each of these enemies Jesus has the answer and has won the victory for us on the cross.

Questions:

1. Where has your greatest battle been as a Christian? How have you been doing in winning that battle?

2. Why is the world at enmity with God [see James 4:4]?

3. What are the three elements of the world that we face according to 1 John 2:16?

OVERCOMING THE WORLD

Bible Reading: 1 John 2:7-29; Romans 12:1-2

Some people have misunderstood the world and see it purely as things and places to avoid. It is in actual fact a spiritual realm that is totally opposed to God. In his epistle John says that if anyone loves the world, the love of the Father is not in them. He goes further and says that nothing in the world comes from the Father [1 John 2:15-17].

One of the titles given to Satan is the prince of this world. Speaking about His death on the cross, Jesus says, "Now is the time for judgment on this world; now the prince of this world will be driven out" [John 12:31].

This world system has no room for the God of the Bible. It has its own system of beliefs and cultures, known as worldviews, and these vary among the different peoples of the world. In J. B. Philips translation we read, "Don't let the world around you squeeze you into its own mould" [Romans 12:2].

The Biblical way to overcome the world and its way of thinking is to have a renewed mind. Romans 12:1 is very clear, "Do not be conformed to this world, but be transformed by the renewing of your mind...."

On our bookstalls there are whole sections of self-help books. These may have some value, but they miss out the dimension of the Spirit who renews the mind. Surely the spiritual renewal of the mind is more than simply self-help, and the danger is that we depend upon what the world says rather than the Holy Spirit.

Most Christians recognize that their thinking should be different, but many seem at a loss as to how to accomplish it. Bringing our lives into line with God's Word will bring about this renewal of our minds and transformation in our lives. If we think on the same things that the world thinks on, we are going to get the same results. If we keep our minds stayed upon God through the study of His Word and fellowship with Him, then we'll have perfect peace [see Isaiah 26:3]. Only when we renew our minds can we enjoy the good, perfect and acceptable will of God. Then we will think with the mind of Christ and overcome the world.

Question:

1. It is so easy to slip into thinking in the way that the world thinks, and especially when we are bombarded with issues in the media. Instead of passively going along with the status quo will you instead seek what God says about these issues in His Word?

2. What steps are you taking to fulfil this injunction of Paul to have a renewed mind?

AN UNDIVIDED MIND

Bible Reading: Matthew 6:19-34; 1 Peter 5:6-11

"Casting all your care upon Him, because He cares for you" [1 Peter 5:7]

Having considered the renewal of the mind as a key to victory over the world, we turn now to the problem of a divided mind. Various times in Scripture we are warned of the danger of a divided mind. James says that a man who doubts is like the waves of the sea that are tossed to and fro and is double-minded. It is because he is double-minded that he is unstable in all his ways [James 1:7-8]. The result of being double minded is instability and unanswered prayers. Later in his epistle James indicates that double-mindedness is sin and that the double-minded man should purify his heart [James 4:8]. So it is also an issue of holiness.

Peter also speaks about double-mindedness but the translators of the Bible called it care. The word translated "care" in 1 Peter 5:7 comes from two Greek words. The first word is 'merimna' from the root word 'meiro' which means 'to divide.' The second Greek word is 'noos' which is translates as 'the mind'. Now hear 1 Peter 5:7 from this different perspective, "Casting all that divides your mind on Him, because He cares for you."

There are times especially in illness that I have struggled between trusting God and looking at my circumstances. Have you struggled in the same way? Isn't it amazing how we get distracted, anxious, and worried when things go wrong or not the way we expect them to work out. It is an issue of double-mindedness and evidence of lack of trust in the Father who loves us and who makes no mistakes. That is why double-mindedness is sin – because it is a lack of faith, and clearly, that which is not from faith is sin [Romans 14:23].

I have discovered that when I specifically repent of this double-mindedness and repeat God's promise in 1 Peter 5:7 back to Him, that trust and peace return.

"Faith came singing into my room, and other guests took flight,

Fear and anxiety, doubt and gloom, Sped out into the night;

I wondered that such peace could be, but faith said simply,

"Don't you see?" Those other guests can't live with me."

A Question:

Is there an area in your life where you have been double-minded? It has hindered faith, caused instability, and made prayer ineffective. Would you bring that now to Jesus, ask for His forgiveness and cleansing and give the burden to Him?

HOW TO DEAL WITH THE FLESH

Bible Reading: Romans 6:1-23; Galatians 5:19-21

The flesh is the world within us. The Greek word translated "flesh" is the word "sarx." Its basic meaning is the self-life, where self, not Jesus, is on the throne of our life. It is the life where "I" am number one and where my will, my way and my desires come first.

Self cannot be **domesticated**. Salvation does not improve self! Christ did not come to improve self but to replace it. Self has no place in God's economy. Self cannot be **disciplined**. However much we try to educate self, expose it to good moral teaching, or change it, self remains wild and deceitful. It is desperately wicked.

Self cannot be **dedicated**. How prone we are to try and do that. The accumulated result of the effort to dedicate self is a system that operates on selfish motivation and selfish rewards. We have in our churches acres and acres of dedicated self [which is not dedication at all]. Self will do anything before it will die. It will pray, work and tithe. It will teach a Sunday school class and become a deacon. It will even preach! It will steep itself in religious tradition to cushion itself against God. As long as self and Christ remain in the same heart there will be a war.

The works of the flesh are clearly stated in Galatians 5:19-21 and are such a contrast to the fruit of the Spirit. We must recognize that we have been [past tense] crucified with Christ [Galatians 2:20], and that when we became His children we died. Listen to Paul's instructions in Romans chapter 6: Consider yourself dead to sin [v11]; Choose not sin [v19]; Choose to obey God [v18].

We choose to allow the Holy Spirit to rule over our minds and our bodies. As we walk in the Spirit, obeying His dictates and leading so we will not fulfill the lusts of the flesh [see Galatians 5:16]. Holiness is living a life of victory over the flesh!

Question:

You may have said that you understand that our old sinful nature was crucified with Christ and that you have sought to follow the steps above to follow the Holy Spirit, but there is a sin that continues to keep you in bondage and prayer does not seem to work. Are you prepared if necessary to seek help to set you free from what may have become a stronghold of the flesh and might even be demonic in nature?

Something to do:

Take time today to praise God and to thank Him for the victory that He has made possible over the sins of the flesh. Ask the Holy Spirit to fill you afresh.

SAY NO TO THE ENEMY

Bible Reading: Ephesians 6:10-20

The devil [meaning "diabolical"] known as satan ["the accuser"], once one of the highest angelic beings, was cast out of heaven because of pride and rebellion and became the enemy of God and of all that God created.

Jesus called this enemy a thief whose purpose is to steal and kill and destroy [John 10:10]. This enemy rules over his kingdom and has a hierarchy of evil forces under him [Ephesians 10:12]. His kingdom is ruled by control and fear.

Satan tempted Eve and Adam in the Garden of Eden and caused them to fall. Satan tempted Jesus in the wilderness to surrender to him, but Jesus said "No" and spoke God's Word to defeat him.

He still attacks today. Sometimes it is very overt and sometimes very subtle. Here are some of the words used in the New Testament to describe how he treats people:

He **ENTICES [Matthew 4:1-11]; DECEIVES [1 Tim. 4:1; 2 Cor. 4:4]; ENSLAVES [Rom. 8:15** – literally "a spirit that makes you a slave"]; **TORMENTS [Matt. 18:34-35; 1 John 4:18]; OPPRESSES [Acts 10:38** – "katadunasteo" = to exercise dominion against; to oppress; to over-burden]; **BINDS [Luke 13:16** – "deo" = to tie up; confine; fasten = with cords that bind]; **HINDERS [1 Thess. 2:18]; BUFFETS [2 Cor. 12:7]** – to buffet = to hit with blow after blow; to punch; to slap; **VEXES** "pascho" [Grk] = to mob, hassle, molest [**Matt. 15:22; 17:15; Luke 6:18; Acts 5:16**]; **TROUBLES [1 Samuel 16:14]**.

The Hebrew word means "to make fearful, afraid, terrify. It speaks of agitation of mind perplexity, uneasiness [see **1 Chron. 10:13-14**]. The NASV translates this as "terrorise."

Compared with our God this enemy is infinitesimally small but he has power to steal, kill and destroy. As he came to Jesus so he will try to tempt and cause you to fall into his trap.

Paul told the Ephesians to stand against this enemy. James exhorts us to resist him and he will flee from us [James 4:7]. "The most important thing that we need to know about Satan is that Jesus defeated him on the cross" [Luther]. We stand in Christ's victory, but must say "No" when the enemy attacks and tempts us. 'No' is a freedom word! I was impressed this week as I found that Jesus used the word 'No' on sixteen separate occasions.

A Prayer:

Thank you Lord Jesus, that you defeated Satan on the cross and that I can enjoy your victory over him. Help me today, however difficult it may be, to say "No" to the evil one's suggestions and temptations. Thank you for Your Name, Your blood and Your Word by which I overcome the evil one today. Amen.

HANG IN THERE – DON'T GIVE UP

Bible Reading: Psalm 37:1-7, 23-27

Have you ever felt tempted to give up! A few days ago, after a wonderful day with the Lord, my guard was down and I walked into a volatile and unexpected situation, where I was publically rebuked and shouted at. The person who did this had neither thought of others nearby who heard the onslaught or my feelings. Perhaps they got out of bed the wrong side!! Perhaps they themselves were hurting because undoubtedly hurt people hurt people! The whole incident left me with an attitude of wanting to give up on these people! Why should I put myself out for them when they attack me like this. In my heart I even began to blame the whole organization and not just the individual.

It would have been so much better if I had not retaliated and risen in anger to the situation. Was it self-defense? Was my pride hurt? Was my response a fleshly and not spiritual response? I think that answer to each of those questions was clearly yes.

It took me a good while to get back my spiritual equilibrium. To apologize and ask forgiveness for my reaction was not difficult but getting over the sense of inner guilt and frustration was far tougher. Why does this sometimes happen, even after seeking to follow Jesus fully for more than fifty years is the deeper question I needed to answer.

Is this experience something that you are familiar with? It took a couple of days to get over, but once again, as I confessed my sin, the blood of Jesus washed me clean and His peace returned. It is a quite a while since I had experienced something like this, but I suddenly realized that this is so relevant to our devotional series on holiness. This is life- we do fall! The Psalmist said that we may stumble....but the Lord upholds us with His hand" [Psalm 37:27]

Don't give up when you fall and don't become depressed when you fail. Get up again, get back to the cross and let the blood of Jesus wash you clean. Remember David's prayer: "Create in me a clean heart, O God, and renew a steadfast spirit within me....Restore to me the joy of your salvation, and grant me a willing spirit, to sustain me" [Psalm 51:10,12].

Questions:

1. If God has spoken personally to you through this devotional, what was it He was saying to you? Is there some action you should take in response to this?

2. There are times when all of us become angry. Some people immediately forgive but don't deal with the deeper inner issues. Some people allow the anger to fester leading to resentment and bitterness. How do you deal with anger?

OUR BLESSED HOPE

Bible Reading: Philippians 3:1-21

It has been a great joy for me to share this series on purity and holiness with you and today we come to a conclusion. What a journey God has brought us on so far. Firstly, when we turned from our sin and received Jesus we were born again of the Holy Spirit and the Holy One made His home in us. He gave us righteousness as a gift and He declared us to be holy in His sight. We became saints, who sometimes sin. We began a journey of holiness, to be filled with God's love and to live a life of beauty. It has been a battle as we have struggled with the world, the flesh and devil. We have gone through discipline and refining fire and pruning, often painful, but the work of a loving God who has been changing us little by little so that we become like His Son, Jesus. This is the journey of a lifetime.

One day we shall see Him face to face, and tell the story saved by grace. When we see Him we shall be like Him. No more sorrow, no more sin, no more tears, no more pain. It will be worth it all when we see Him.

Writing whilst under house arrest in Rome, the apostle Paul reveals the passion in his heart that continued to burn like a fire. He says, that he has not yet attained to the goal or reached perfection but that he is pressing toward the day when he will finally be all that Jesus Christ saved him for and wants him to be. He leaves the past behind and strains forward towards the prize for which God, through Christ Jesus, was calling him up to heaven. We join him and the saints who have gone before us on this journey of purity and holiness.

A Question:

There have been many issues raised as we have looked at the meaning of holiness. What has the Lord been specifically saying to you over these past weeks?

Something to Do:

Why not begin a journal? Begin to write each day what God says to you and what He teaches you. It may seem insignificant in the beginning, but one day you will read back in amazement and see how God has been leading you. All it needs is a notebook, a pencil and a few minutes each day.

About the author - Michael Ross-Watson

Converted to Christianity in 1963 from a family background of Spiritism, Michael attended Cliff College and worked as a lay evangelist in the Methodist Church (UK) from 1966 to 1969. He and his wife, Esther, have served with WEC International (Worldwide Evangelization for Christ) from 1969 until the present time. They served for ten years as missionaries in Indonesia. Michael has been ministering internationally as an evangelist and teacher since 1982.

Much of Michael's ministry has been in Singapore and particularly the Anglican Church of our Saviour, where he was appointed as honorary pastor.

Michael and Esther are members of the Kerith Community Church in Bracknell, England.

You can read more daily devotionals from Michael at his blog

MichaelRossWatson.com

Also in the Climbing Higher Daily Readings Series

Proverbs – One thought for the day taken from a section of each chapter of Proverbs

Eternity – What happens to us when we die and how can we prepare ourselves now.

Christmas – Taken mainly from the four gospel accounts in the New Testament. Why did Jesus come into the world? What does Christmas mean to you today?

Bonus Chapter from Climbing Higher Daily Readings – Book 2

Proverbs – Daily Readings from the book of Proverbs

THE FEAR OF THE LORD

Bible Reading: Proverbs 1:1-32

As we begin a new series in Proverbs we will take a key verse from each chapter in Proverbs. We are beginning with what is possibly the key verse of the whole Book of Proverbs:

"The fear of the Lord is the beginning of knowledge" [Proverbs 1:7]

The phrase "the fear of the Lord" is found many times in the Bible but is possibly one of the most misunderstood of phrases. Many times I have been asked why God wants us to be afraid of Him. That is not the meaning of the phrase "the fear of the Lord." This fear is not a bad fear but has the meaning of reverence and respect.

The fear of the Lord is the awesome respect and reverence for the person of the Lord and His authority. This reverence for the Lord is the beginning of knowledge. The word beginning means "the first principle" but can also mean "the first step towards" – literally the first step to grow in the knowledge of the Lord is to have reverence for Him.

The fear of the Lord is to shun, hate and avoid sin [Proverbs 8:13; 3:7; 16:6]. When we have a right attitude and relationship with God we will hate sin. In this sense the fear of the Lord is protective, because it keeps us from sin.

The fear of the Lord is life-giving [Proverbs 14:27] and adds to the length of life [Proverbs 10:27]. It also leads to peace and contentment - "The fear of the LORD leads to life: Then one rests content, untouched by trouble" [Proverbs 19:23]. This rightful reverence for God, together with humility, brings both wealth and honour, as well as life [Proverbs 22:4].

The fear of the Lord is a choice that we make! In Proverbs 1:29 we read that God will not answer or be found of those who did not choose to fear the Lord.

The writer of Proverbs exhorts us not to be envious of sinners, but to always be zealous for the fear of the Lord [Proverbs 23:17].

Let's choose to submit to God, obey Him and choose to reverence Him.

Questions:

1. What is the evidence that a person fears the Lord?

2. Why is the fear of the Lord so important to the Christian?

3. How would you explain to someone who doesn't understand the meaning of what the fear of the Lord is?

Printed in Great Britain
by Amazon.co.uk, Ltd.,
Marston Gate.